248   216
Bre

AUTHOR
Brenner, Henry

TITLE The art of living joyfully

248   216
Bre

Brenner -   The art of living
                joyfully.

THE ART OF LIVING JOYFULLY

Printed by the Abbey Press, St. Meinrad, Indiana, U.S.A.

The
Art
Of
Living
Joyfully

by

Henry Brenner, O.S.B.

AUTHOR OF
THE COURAGEOUS SHALL CONQUER
SEEK AND YOU SHALL FIND

**THE GRAIL
ST. MEINRAD, INDIANA**

Imprimi Potest

✠ Ignatius Esser, O.S.B.

Nihil Obstat

Cyril Gaul, O.S.B.

Imprimatur

✠ Joseph Ritter, D.D.

Feast of Our Lady of Einsiedeln, 1942

SECOND EDITION

Fifth Printing 1945

CHAPTERS

(For Index by Topics, see page 138.)

THE ART
OF
LIVING JOYFULLY

Chapter 1

"ASK MY HORSE!"

The spirit of serenity shows self-control. Our Savior possessed this spirit—we are speaking of His human nature—in a marked degree. For St. Mark tells us that Pilate wondered at His self-composure under accusation. "And Pilate again asked him, saying: 'Hast thou no answer to make? Behold how many things they accuse thee of.' But Jesus made no further answer, so that Pilate wondered." (15.4)

One of the four cardinal virtues is temperance; and it is this virtue which forms the mainspring of serenity. In our modern age of haste and unrest, it is considered rather old-fashioned to advocate temperance

1

in its true meaning of entire self-control. For we have become accustomed to the opposite—immoderate yielding to desires, unrestrained freedom of appetites and desires. Yet, if we stop to ponder seriously, we see that such freedom is like that of a runaway horse. It reminds us of the old story, which tells of a horse and his rider, galloping at full speed; a bystander, amazed at the wild sight, cried to the rider: "Where are you going?" The answer was: "Don't ask me; ask my horse." It was Raphael who depicted Temperance holding a horse's bridle.

Excessive worry, be it in regard to business, public affairs, housekeeping, legislation, or anything else, is like a devil forever goading us on to all sorts of foolish notions, outlandish resolves, and ridiculous deeds. Temperate zeal is always in place; but if it grows intemperate, it leads to error. Care about the present, past, or future, if it is moderate, makes us better and happier; but if immoderate, it plunges us into confusion and misery.

One of the greatest hindrances to the attainment of personal peace and self-control, is to suppose that it is out of one's reach.

"ASK MY HORSE!"

We are inclined to say: "If things were only different, then I could be different; but the way they are, I have little hope." Let us remember, peace can be had in the midst of trouble, if we confide in God. We make the mistake of thinking that things have to change before we can change; whereas the truth is, if we ourselves could only change—from self-centeredness to divine confidence—then the exterior things would change—from miseries to delights, for they would be suffered and offered up to God in the spirit of true Christian resignation. Did not St. Paul say: "Now we know that for those who love God all things work together unto good"? (Rom. 8.28) He makes no exception—"all things" is his promise.

Losses, real or feared, often disconcert us and are the cause of endless worry and misery as a consequence. How false a view of life! Losses are often our secret opportunities. Considered from one angle, the loss we suffer is indeed a misfortune; but from another angle, it is a blessing. The world lost Christ on Calvary; but thereby it gained salvation. "God knows best" is always the most reliable consoler in human set-backs. He knows how to give us something better!

St Augustine's definition of peace—"the tranquillity of order"—remains the best solution of earth's difficulties. For, as St. Paul says, "if God is for us, who is against us?" (Rom. 8.31) If our soul remains in good order with God, what harm can the alterations occuring in other things do to us? We ourselves do not change—we are in order, always resigned to God's will; if other things get out of order, they themselves change, but we remain unchanged. We therefore enjoy not only order, but the tranquillity of order, which St. Augustine calls "peace." And that tranquillity solves all our problems—regularly and faithfully.

Chapter 2

A BALANCED PERSONALITY

The placid soul is ready for all things; even in the face of death it does not lose its control over self; as Jesus, who at His last breath commended His spirit into His Father's hands. "And Jesus cried out with a loud voice and said: 'Father, into thy hands I commend my spirit.' And having said this, he expired." (Luke 23.46)

To be placid signifies two things, to have a good conscience, which belongs to the will, and a tranquil thought-life, which belongs to the mind. A person may have the one without the other. There are many good people who try their best to avoid any offense against God, but who are continually worrying in their mind about this and about that. Just so, there are many tranquil-minded people, who refuse to be worried about anything, but who care little or nothing about the will of God; they are mere Stoics.

A balanced personality has both one and the other: a good conscience, and a calm mind. Such a person aims not only at doing no wrong, but also at making no mistake. And indeed, happiness, in its true meaning, cannot be present without this combination. The soul cannot be happy unless it is joined to God's holy will, but it cannot reach this state unless it is careful to avoid getting on the wrong road, be it in this or be it in that. We know the old saying, that hell is paved with good intentions.

Often it is our work which proves the occasion for our lack of mental placidity. Instead of going forward with it and trying to enjoy it, as being the will of God for us, or at least the source of our up-keep, we fret and grow impatient, and allow the mere exterior phases of that work to annoy us and continually keep us dissatisfied. This may happen even with a person who recognizes in his work a most sacred obligation which he is determined to carry out at all times. His conscience is placid, but his mind—it may be surprisingly disturbed. Such a half-happiness is what causes many ailments—nervous conditions especially, for which remedy after remedy is tried, without ever arriving at the cause, and therefore without ever reaching a real cure. Such a person ought to seek the proper balance; not only to do the will of God, but to do it as God wants it done, which certainly is not in anxiety and the spirit of distaste, but in cool-headedness and the spirit of acquiescence. God is not satisfied with only half of us—the will, but He wants the other half, too—our mind.

How to do this best often depends on practical circumstances. A person with heavy physical work is not going to make that work more tasteful by relaxation in the form of added physical strain; some calm mental work would give him just the relaxation he needs. On the other hand, a person with heavy mental obligations is not going to make those obligations more pleasant to himself by seeking recreation in additional mental strain; what he needs is some healthy physical relaxation. "Variety delights," says the old proverb.

Blaming others for our own dissatisfaction is another common trait in our human make-up. In fact, we often grow so attached to this particular kind of disturbance, that we are annoyed even at the sight of someone. How many serious disorders this causes in family life is evidenced by the numberless divorces of our modern age. Gilbert K. Chesterton once remarked that with many the "through my fault" of the Confiteor ought really to be, "through his or her fault," for in the heart there is no real self-accusation, but rather a weak, misery-breeding self-excusing at the expense of someone else.

Chapter 3

FLASHLIGHTS

A Christian's countenance and heart ought to remain in control always; unjust anger Christ threatened with judgment, that is, with punishment. " 'But I say to you that everyone who is angry with his brother shall be liable to judgment.' " (Matt. 5.22).

Anger is an irritation. If some part of the body is irritated by continual friction, it becomes sore; if something is not done about it, serious results may be expected. In the same manner, repeated acts of irritation where the mind or soul are concerned will eventually end in distress. Some are ready at the slightest provocation to yield to anger; perhaps not in a visible way, nor even consciously to themselves, but the irritation is there nevertheless. And this constant irritation wears; it uses up the reserve energy of both soul and body. It may be compared to the action of a thoughtless boy, who repeatedly pushes the button on his flashlight; he thinks only of the light, not of the wear on the batteries.

Consider the day of a person easily subject to irritation. Although the alarm clock is a most faithful servant, he feels offended at its sudden call, and shuts it off in a mood of peevishness. He rises in that mood, and the least little happening out of the ordinary, such as the dropping of a collar button, only increases the condition. Instead of blaming self for the situation, the old excuse is reverted to—"I must have got out on the wrong side of the bed." He goes to breakfast, expecting his favorite cereal, but finds something that does not appeal to his taste. As he arrives at the office, the first thing he does is to scold the stenographer for not having things immediately ready for his perusal. That settled, an agent announces himself; another irritation. The agent has hardly seated himself, when the telephone rings; still another irritation. Thus the day wears on, and—wears him out: no, rather he himself wears himself out.

Can such a condition be corrected? The poor mortal has accustomed himself to it by habit; he could also accustom himself to the opposite by habit. Let him only try. Instead of yielding to tension at the crucial moment, let him relax; instead of knitting his brow in a frown, let him curl his lips in a smile; instead of seeing everything in the dark light, let him view each circumstance in the bright light. In fact, let him cease making everything that comes along so important that he must lose his temper over it; on the contrary, let him learn how to pass over insignificant things as just little milestones on his way. As to the important things, let him take his time, consider the matter carefully, and coolly attend to it, then go to the next thing. He will thus be like a man, whose flashlight is used when it should be used, and in the right way; not like a silly boy, whose only object is to pass the time away.

When anger grows violent, then its victim is nothing more than a wild beast, treacherous, dangerous, unreliable, and very unpleasant to deal with. A chronic ailment renders a man sick enough; but when he runs a high temperature, anything may happen. A mad bull running loose in a china shop pictures such a one excellently. Only he is worse than a bull—he has a will of his own, which remains, even though he is forced to give in.

Chapter 4

THE DIVINE PHYSICIAN

To be patient means, to suffer something that hinders or hurts us, and still retain our self-composure. Our Savior's patience was wonderful; they struck His face and even spat on it. "Then they spat in his face and buffeted him; while others struck his face with the palms of their hands." (Matt. 26.67).

How many difficulties, with their consequent unpleasantness and discord, could be smoothed over and almost entirely eliminated by patience! But so many of us are so adverse to suffering anything, that we even think it wrong to do so. To put up with another's ill manners seems to us a degradation of our own personality—a weakening of our character. How utterly false! No; patience always elevates us personally and strengthens our character; the only exception is, when patience would

mean connivance, that is, a culpable neglect of evident duty. Heli, as we read
in Holy Writ, was so patient with his way-
ward sons, that he did not even correct
them; this was culpable, not virtuous, and
God punished him accordingly. Patience,
in its virtuous meaning, is something quite
different; generally, it is the virtue to be
practiced, when we are personally offended
at something, and where annoyance at it
would neither do the offender good nor
benefit our own soul.

But we need patience not only with
others, we need it also with ourselves. In
sickness this is especially true. In the first
place, we must avoid fearing sickness too
much. A person may become very unhappy
and full of nervous anxiety by such an attitude toward the physical vicissitudes of
life. If we look back upon our lives, we
must acknowledge that very few of the
serious illnesses that we thought were
going to strike us, ever did. And probably
the ones that did strike us proved a blessing, not an evil, so that whenever we think
of them we simultaneously think of the
proverb. " 'Tis an ill wind that blows no
man good."

14

THE DIVINE PHYSICIAN

Pains are an asset in our physical account; they tell us in time, if there is any danger ahead. Unless they are severe, we may simply observe quietly and wait; if they grow in intensity, we may see a physician. If we really become sick, we may hope for the best, not the worst. Our faith will help us here above all else. For God is a physician who not only knows just exactly what is the matter with us, but who can so arrange matters that we get just the right remedy. He need not work a miracle to save us, but all He needs to do is to suggest to the physician who has us in charge what medicine or treatment to give us, and the trouble will soon clear up. Some make the mistake of always expecting a miracle when they pray to God in sickness. What is the use of a miracle when some natural means, which He has already created, can turn the trick? Let us pray for that, and He will not deprive us of it; the box of pills that our human physician prescribes we may then look upon not just as another box of pills, but as a special gift of God Himself, who is both all-knowing and all-powerful, something which cannot be said of any human physician.

Chapter 5

WHAT OF YOUR SUFFERINGS?

Christ exhorted us to suffer even persecution with patience. " 'Blessed are they who suffer persecution for justice' sake, for theirs is the kingdom of heaven.' " (Matt. 5.10). He gave us an example that showed us how to bear up with trials. "And plaiting a crown of thorns, they put it upon his head, and a reed into his right hand; and bending the knee before him they mocked him, saying, 'Hail, King of the Jews!' and they spat on him, and took the reed and kept striking him on the head." (Matt. 27. 29,30)

When trials and sufferings are just passing and soon abate, or at least may be expected to do so, it is not so hard to bear up with them; but when they continue, even in the face of all our efforts to remedy them, then the difficulty becomes much greater. If the soldiers had struck our

Lord once or twice with the reed, it would have been different; but we are told that they "kept striking him on the head." That is just what happens to us and what is often the source of our rebellion and even revenge. It may be something around us, like a person, or a condition, like a grating noise; or it may be something in us ourselves, like a sickness, or an infirmity. How can we remain happy in such circumstances?

Here are a few thoughts that may help us to go through such sufferings with a minimum of annoyance. They are spiritual thoughts for the most part. Above all, we must remember that our Savior looked upon sufferings borne for God, and as sent or allowed by God, not as curses but as blessings. Why? Because our sins are thus expiated already in this life; yes, out of sufferings often sprout the finest flowers and fruits of virtue. The Blessed Virgin Mary had her share of sufferings—we call her the Sorrowful Mother—and by bearing them perfectly she showed herself our model and comfortress. If one uses these spiritual goads of faith with habitual care and earnestness, a wonderful thing will

17

begin to develop; the soul will actually find
in the naturally sorrowful trials supernatural joys—joys which excel all the joys
that men crave. And when one turns from
time and puts the mind only on eternity,
the additional reminder of everlasting
merit increases those joys immeasurably.
Suffering, viewed in this light, is something
quite other than what it is commonly considered to be; instead of a ghastly spectre
of ill-boding and misery, it takes on the
aspect of an angel of God, full of love and
high purpose. It is therefore not feared
as an enemy, but respected and treasured
as a friend.

There have been Saints who have prayed
for sufferings. This seems altogether
drastic and uncalled-for to many people.
But we must remember that such holy
souls were so completely wrapped up in
God and in the future life, that they were
spiritually avaricious and longed to heap
up as much merit for themselves in the
after life as they possibly could; or, they
did not even think of themselves—it was
their supreme purpose to love God as much
as possible, and they could think of no better way to prove this love than to ask for

hardships (always of course presupposing the will of God), for love is superior to difficulty, it overcomes all things for the sake of the beloved, and is so anxious to show its willingness, that it goes in search of occasions.

Chapter 6

OUR COMPANION

Tranquillity is the natural companion of a good conscience and of the consequent trust in God which marks those who possess it. Our Lord told us to remain tranquil even under persecution. " 'And when they bring you before the synagogues and the magistrates and the authorities, do not be anxious how or wherewith you shall defend yourselves, or what you shall say, for the Holy Spirit will teach you in that very hour what you ought to say.' " (Luke 12. 11,12)

A lake is said to be tranquil when the atmosphere is quiet and no breeze or wind disturbs its surface. Then it reflects the landscape and sky like a mirror and excites the admiration of every eye that views it. Even so the soul of man, when tranquillity reigns over it, reflects everything on earth and in heaven without distortion, and is truly admirable to observe. Look at the faces of Raphael's Madonnas; there you see not countenances so much as the human soul, at rest, in control of itself, and reflecting the finer things of life with wonderful precision.

Worry generally has its seat in some form of persecution, feared by the individual, who, like a bird, is ever looking this way and that for a possible enemy. Some are persecuted by the thought that they will lose what they have or not obtain what they need. Instead of trusting in God and remaining calm, they allow themselves to fall into a perpetual upheaval. Some again worry so much about the temporal that they neglect the eternal. Still others worry to the point that, in order not to be caught napping, they go to dishonest extremes and provide for themselves even against the commandment of God, 'Thou shalt not steal.' Finally, some worry so much about eternity, that they forget that they are living in time, and permit foolish scrupulosity to dictate their course of life. All these are self-sufficient, lacking confidence in God.

In our modern age the fear of not finishing in time what we are doing saps the spiritual, mental, and bodily strength of many. Such are always in a stew: if they ride, they must always get there as quickly as possible; if they wait, they must forever pull out their watches, to see how far behind schedule they are; if they eat—well, they never eat, they just swallow; if they expect, they must think of nothing else, do nothing else, until the expected happens; if it happens, they are nervous with elation, or they must take a rest, to make up for the energy spent and give their nerves a chance to recuperate; if it does not happen, they are disconsolate, and their expectancy turns sour—into chagrin, disgust, peevishness, and a pitiful self-coddling.

When a person once begins to fear the consequences of over-wrought fear, then he is on the road to true tranquillity. His eyes begin to see things in their right perspective; his soul is alive to the fact that it was created for something more than these mere passing vicissitudes. He begins to take hold of his better self, as it were, and place it on the pedestal which heretofore he reserved for his worse self. He becomes an adorer of God's will, not a worshipper of his own 'ego.' In a word, he pulls up the shade, opens the window, and lets in the sunshine of God's Providence.

Job said: "Although he should kill me, I will trust in him." (13.15) And indeed, what else did the holy martyrs do? They tranquilly gave up their very lives, knowing that they would receive something infinitely better in return. For what is this present life in itself alone? Truly a warfare and a vale of tears. But looked at as a journey to the better life beyond, it becomes truly a potential triumph and eternal victory.

Chapter 7

THE BLESSED MAN OF PSALM I

Our Lord desired that we have peace of
heart. "Now while they were talking of
these things, Jesus stood in their midst,
and said to them, 'Peace to you! It is I,
do not be afraid.'" (Luke 24.36) He also
reminded us that we cannot find this true
peace in the turmoil of the world but only
in a virtuous interior. "'Peace I leave with
you, my peace I give to you; not as the
world gives do I give to you. Do not let
your heart be troubled, or be afraid.'"
(John 14.27)

Never was there a better description
written of the human heart at peace than
that set down by the inspired writer in
the first psalm: "Blessed is the man."
Eight qualities or marks are there enu-
merated. The first is: "Who hath not
walked in the counsel of the ungodly." We
moderns are confirmed readers of every-

thing and anything that we lay our hands upon. We rely on our good judgment to keep at least our hearts aloof from what is evil. But, as the old saying warns us, it is difficult to touch pitch without some of it sticking to our fingers. Without our realizing it, misleading counsel is bound here and there to steal into our interior, and, like poison in the body, have an evil effect in our soul. Before, we had no doubt about our position; now, we must combat with the other fellow's opinion, even though we do not believe it: before, we knew only the counsel of the godly, now, we know also that of the ungodly. Like our first parents, we now know the difference between good and evil, and the dogs of war, though as yet only whelps, are let loose in the depths of our subconscious self.

The second mark of the peaceful man, according to the psalmist, is: "Nor stood in the way of sinners." If we care nothing about occasions of sin, are we not plainly standing in the way of sinners? We may not give in to the sin, but the stench thereof is in our nostrils, and it robs us of that clean, sweet air which those breathe who wisely keep clear of occasions.

The third mark is: "Nor sat in the chair of pestilence." Did the psalmist perhaps, in a prophetic vision, here foretell our modern picture shows? Verily, the people sitting there in those darkened dens of all that is savage and degrading in human nature, can often be said to have paid for a "chair of pestilence." And even though they remain uncontaminated, still they carry away the disturbing memory of something which perhaps they were entirely ignorant of before.

The fourth mark is positive: "His will is in the law of the Lord." How many of us are so determined to do God's will that nothing can keep us from doing it? Many have their private idols, though they sing the "Credo" as loudly as the rest. And those idols, every time they are seen, rob their owners of some of that joy which is proper to the true servants of God. Secretly those owners hear that voice of the Apocalypse saying: "Thou holdest fast my name, and hast not denied my faith.... But I have against thee a few things." (2.

13,14) They answer with Adam, signifi-
cantly: "I heard thy voice ... and I was
afraid." (Gen. 3.10)

The fifth mark is also positive, very
much so: "And on his law he shall medi-
tate day and night." If we pass a half
hour in church services or in meditative
thought without going to sleep, we think
we have done a wonder. How the rest of
the day is spent is a matter hard to decide
—it is a mixture perhaps of everything
possible with some few good and holy
thoughts scattered here and there like
needles in a hay stack. As to the night,
perhaps we do not even say our night
prayers; or spend our time in drink,
games, or worse, till the wee hours of the
morning. We have not even a peaceful
night's rest; dissipation gnaws at our soul
like a worm in the wood, and even though
we see it not, it is there.

The sixth mark points out the effect:
"He shall be like a tree which is planted
near the running waters, which shall bring
forth its fruit, in due season." Our religious duties and privileges are like running
waters, always ready to refresh us, and
bring forth the fruit—good works. Are

we near them, or at a distance from them? In them is true peace—away from them uncertainty and uneasiness reign.

The seventh mark is: "And his leaf shall not fall off." Are we consistently good, faithful and determined? Or do we live in spurts and bounds, one while imitating the saints, another playing games with the demon? And how about order in our daily duties? Are we procrastinators, putting off and piling up work, then attacking the result with a vehemence that robs us of all calm and peace? Procrastinators are never happy.

Finally, the eighth mark puts the crown upon all the rest: "And all whatsoever he shall do shall prosper." Prosperity means progress, success, well-being. The man with true peace in his heart is always progressing; he is always succeeding; he is always well, spiritually healthy, and full of joy: not, however, as the world sees progress, success and well-being, but as God, the Light Uncreated, the Light Eternal, the Light Most Holy sees it. "Not as the world gives do I give to you."

To sum up this chapter: our peace of heart would be much greater, if we watched more wisely over our reading, were more viligant regarding occasions, more selective in our amusements, more attached to the will of God, more faithful to our religious and other duties, and more appreciative of our opportunities.

Chapter 8

"REMEMBER LOT'S WIFE"

Lot's wife was not composed; she could not refrain from looking back in her nervous curiosity. (Gen. 19) Our Lord told us to remember her. "'Remember Lot's wife.'" (Luke 17.32)

Some years ago a young man, blind from his second year, celebrated his twenty-second year, thanks to modern medical science, by regaining his sight. Asked about his impressions on such an extraordinary occasion, he replied: "I have had a great disappointment in seeing human faces. My ideal was far too high, and in a way I had to go down a lot ... I imagined all faces were peaceful."

If a person stops a moment and tries to 'feel' his own face, he will suddenly realize things that perhaps never before struck him. Especially the frown on his forehead makes him cognizant of something hereto-

fore entirely ignored—tension. If he tries
this especially at night time when he is
trying to go to sleep, he will be surprised
at the 'ropes' pulling down around his skull.
Relaxing them is not so easy a matter;
and to keep them relaxed, he will find a
difficult matter, for those muscles are so accustomed to tension that as soon as they
can they go right back to their usual state.

In all excitement there is tension. At
times, we cannot help but be in such a
state; our nervous system is so constituted.
Healthy tension is strength. But to be
habitually on tension is very detrimental,
both physically and mentally, and it is a
part of wisdom to live a relaxed existence
as far as possible. All the muscular parts
of the body are here concerned. If relaxation is the rule, then when tension is needed
it can be exercised with great strength and
profit; but if tension is the rule, then when
relaxation is needed, great difficulty is
liable to be experienced; instead of getting
one's needed rest, the time is spent in
wasted effort—sleep comes only by exhaus-
tion. A man's habits make or unmake him;
and what he spends habitually decides the
status of his fortune. One man will spend

a great amount of energy on something, whereon another works very economically; often the economist will be found to accomplish the matter more quickly and efficiently than the spendthrift. For cool control is always better than excessive excitement, at least in the long run.

The Christian's composure grows on him, in accord with the progress of his belief and trust in God's care for him. It is the simple confidence of the little child, which, as long as it is clinging to its mother's apron, feels safe and free from fear. Its mother, it knows, is both powerful enough to protect it, and has love for it enough to go to any sacrifice in carrying out that protection. All it has to do is to keep close to its mother, and that loving, watchful mother will do the rest.

We are all children of God. If we keep close to Him, by observing His commandments and trusting in His promises, why need we be always living under the stress of fear and useless excess of energy? Such a course of action is very illogical, just as it would be illogical for the child to distrust its mother. Therefore, the holy simplicity of our Christian faith is worth more to us than anything else on this troubled earth. If we only let its salutary influence guide and surround us, we can and must lead a life full of the least possible disturbance and rich in the greatest possible self-control. It will be said of us as it is said of God Himself: "But thou being master of power, judgest with tranquillity." (Wis. 12.18)

Chapter 9

POSSESSORS OF THE EARTH

The most Christlike virtue has a promise from the Savior's lips. He said that the meek shall come into possession of the land, that is,—and above all,— save their souls in eternity. " 'Blessed are the meek: for they shall possess the earth.' " (Matt. 5.4)

A barrier stands before meekness; that barrier is the mistaken conception that it is a virtue displaying weakness rather than strength. It is looked upon as revealing a tame, yielding character, a person without any strength of conviction, a coward whom the brave handle as they will. This view would change the words of our Savior to: "Blessed are the angry; for they are the ones who shall possess the earth."

To show the falsity of this view it is only necessary to call attention to the fact that a meek man is like a well-armed man who uses his weapons only when it is just and reasonable. For meekness does not rob a man of the power of anger, but only regulates it, keeps it in control, and ennobles it. Moses is praised as a most meek man, but we know what strength he showed on the occasion of the golden calf, just as Christ afterward overthrew the tables of the money-changers in the temple—He who said of Himself: "I am meek and humble of heart." (Matt. 11.29)

The meek man controls himself, and self-control is strength. The passionate man does not control himself, and lack of self-control is weakness. Besides, the meek man is able to correct others with discretion, where the passionate man only makes matters worse. The meek man has a reputation of being tolerant and reasonable; the passionate man is shunned as an intolerant fanatic and detested as an unreasonable bully. The meek man does not seek revenge; whereas vengeance is the first thing a passionate man thinks of, once he in thwarted. The meek man, finally, preserves fraternal charity, even when he must use just anger, and, according to the Gospel, he loves his enemies; but the passionate

man cares nothing about charity, and hates
his enemies, often with a mortal hatred,
satisfied like Cain with nothing less than
blood.

The effect of meekness on the human
system in general is like that of oil—it
soothes and heals. This is true whether
we consider the one who practices meekness or those who are its recipients. How
much trouble a meek man can save himself
in the course of a lifetime! And what
worlds of trouble do not gather by and by
in the lives of those who perpetually bubble
over with passion!

Meekness is especially very good for the
health of the body; for it enables the reserve energy to accumulate, even as money
in a bank, and to be in readiness for any
emergency. It makes a man feel good; he
has pleasant memories: he can even think
of his enemies with pleasure, for he has
not, like the fool in the proverb, rubbed the
old sore! It causes his friends to multiply
continually: the old ones grow more friendly and the new ones cling to him as to a
rare treasure. And when the time comes
when he needs a friend, he will find not
one, but many.

In fine, meekness is an all-around medicine, tonic, and stimulant. It will help a man to live a longer life than all the good food and beverages in the world. Its investments are better than money; its dividends greater than riches; its affluence and influence more extensive than royalty and power.

Chapter 10

LAMBS AMONG WOLVES

Our Lord did not excuse His disciples from the practice of mildness even by reason of hindering circumstances; for He told them that He would send them forth as lambs among wolves. " 'Behold I send you as lambs in the midst of wolves.' " (Luke 10.3)

We speak of a mild day, when the temperature is pleasant, the sky is bright, the breeze gentle, and the whole face of nature in a state of restful calm. There is no excess of heat or cold, no storminess of atmosphere, no threatening clouds, no depressive feeling in the air. An ideal day, we say, and the pleasure we derive therefrom goes over into everything we do, say, and think. We are in a good humor, feel fine, and the world seems quite a different world after all.

How easy it is to feel fine on such a day!
To go through such a day, and call it a perfect one at the end, is no proof that we ourselves are mild and gentle. No; to prove
that we must be able to go through just the
opposite, and still feel in a good humor.
That is true mildness. For no virtue is
genuine until it has been tried and not
found wanting.

Nor do mild actions, mild words, and
mild thoughts, constitute mildness. All of
us, on occasion, can be the very incarna-
tion of mildness. How the little child,
when it desires something very much, can
approach its mother and act as if it were
an angel; sweet words flow from its lips, en-
dearing signs of love and filial piety break
forth from its whole being. And how
gracious an agent can be who has in mind
to make a sale! What honeyed words he
uses, how pleasant is his countenance, how
wonderful his patience!

Yes, mildness of policy is something
quite different from mildness of disposition. It is the latter that is really worthy
of the name. It alone goes through one's
life like a golden thread and joins all things
together in one garland of joy and healthy

zeal. It alone has a true and lasting foundation—humility, the virtue that knows how to 'take it' personally, the virtue so enamored of the mild and gentle Savior, whose presence so drew others about Him.

If the mild man thinks, he avoids rash judgment, and always puts the best interpretation possible on others' actions; if he speaks, he is careful not to detract, and when he must correct others, he does so with the least possible offense; if he writes a letter, he is intent on conveying to the other a mood of satisfaction and pleasure; if he has any dealings with his neighbor, he makes a point of observing the rules of etiquette and decency, abhorring anything that may make him offensive or put others ill at ease. In a word, the mild man lives in a world where God's sunshine is always shining; indeed, he is like a sun himself, whose rays go forth and enlighten dark corners and warm cold breasts.

The demon does not want us to be mild; he always suggests harshness and severity. However, he is careful to cover up his insidious advice with the argument of justice. He says: "It is all very well to be mild; but does your duty allow it?" Thus

he intrigues us into using sarcasm, which
cuts, ridicule, which offends, and cruel
vituperation, which antagonizes. Afterwards, he laughs at us, and we ourselves,
realizing how we have been duped, feel—as
we commonly say—like kicking ourselves.
But we are so slow to learn. We could
know our best procedure here, but we are
forever going off to the right and left, instead of remaining on the golden middle
way.

Chapter 11

THE DEEP VIRTUE

Calmness depends on self-control, which enables a man to remain master of himself under the most trying circumstances. Our Lord expressed it by saying that patience keeps the soul unharmed and unshaken. " 'By your patience you will win your souls.' " (Luke 21.19)

Calmness is a deep virtue; it penetrates the soul to its very bottom. Patience is its inseparable companion; if patience forsakes it but a moment, it begins immediately to wilt, like a flower nipped by the frost. A person who possesses it habitually, is a happy mortal indeed; for he is proof against all manner of disquietude. Many do possess it in a way, that is, as long as nothing extraordinary happens; but then they find it very difficult to hold, even with the best of will and desire. The reason is, because it has much to do with

the nerves, which are so constituted that
they are always ready to tremble, like
leaves in a breeze.

To be calm is one thing; to try to be
calm is another. Most of us have to be
satisfied with the latter; and it is no mean
satisfaction, for continual practice will
gradually make perfect. But we must remember one phase of the matter, which is
this: to rely purely on natural means, as
psychologists often do, furnishes only part
of what is possible; it is faith that comple-
ments the natural—faith in the divine power, that power which Christ Himself used
in quelling the turbulent waves.

A beautiful and instructive story is told
of Pope Pius XI concerning a little picture
of Christ calming the waves. It is best told
in the great Pontiff's own words, which
follow: "I found it the first day I set foot
in what was to be my future workroom. I
had just been elected to the Pontificate.
My mind was filled with the most weighty
preoccupations concerning the formidable
responsibility which Divine Providence had
seen fit to place upon my shoulders. I certainly had full faith in the help of the
Heavenly Father, but I felt weighted down

under the heavy office entrusted to me. I
entered the great room and found it empty
and full of dust. I approached the big table which occupied the middle and saw
there, as though abandoned by chance, that
picture. I took it and kept it. I thanked
the Heavenly Father from the depth of my
heart and felt quieter; more complete and
serene faith filled my heart. I wished that
the little picture should from that moment
watch over every act of my pontificate. I
had it placed in a modest frame and from
then on, on my work-table it stands. Every
time anxiety or grief assails me, every
time a more difficult or painful circumstance presents itself in my ministry, I
look at that picture and the sight of it
renews in me that sense of faith which
consoled me so much in the first twilight
of my pontificate."

His was a great soul; yet it was a humble, believing soul. It was not he who was
going to guide the Church, to deal with
the whole world, to write those great en-
cyclicals, to spend seventeen years full of
the most arduous and admirable labors for
the honor and glory of God and the salvation of souls: no, it was not he, it was the

Master Himself, whose humble tool he had become. It was faith in God that sustained him through all those trying years, calm in his greatness, mighty in his calmness.

A man ought therefore to look upon the spirit of calmness rather as a gift from God than an acquisition to be gotten by one's own endeavors, even though he himself must do his part. Elias the Prophet, as we read in the 19th chapter of the Third Book of Kings, "went forward, one day's journey into the desert. And when he was there, and sat under a juniper tree, he requested for his soul that he might die, and said: It is enough for me, Lord, take away my soul: for I am not better than my fathers. And he cast himself down, and slept in the shadow of the juniper tree: and behold an angel of the Lord touched him, and said to him: Arise and eat. He looked, and behold there was at his head a hearth cake, and a vessel of water: and he ate and drank, and he fell asleep again. And the angel of the Lord came again the second time, and touched him, and said to him: Arise, eat: for thou hast yet a great way to go. And he arose, and ate, and drank, and walked in the strength of that food forty days and forty nights, unto the mount of God, Horeb." Certainly, whatever that food and drink were, they were excellent figures of the calm which enables a man, despite weighing troubles, to go forward and—while he thought he was at his rope's end—find to his amazement that he has "yet a great way to go," and—what is still more amazing—that he actually accomplishes the seemingly impossible, and goes that way!

Calmness is like a pearl, which is taken up out of the ocean depths, where everything is at peace and free from the turbulent vicissitudes of the surface; that pearl is a treasure, and while the fisherman must go after it, it is the divine hand that is going to guide him to it and bring him safely back with it.

Chapter 12

THE WAR HORSE

Our Lord gave us a brilliant example of self-possession when the bold servants struck Him and mocked Him; for He remained calm and unmoved. "And the men who had him in custody began to mock him and beat him . . . , saying, 'Prophesy, who is it that struck thee.' " (Luke 22.63,64)

Sudden happenings will destroy the equilibrium of even the most even-natured individuals. If such an unlooked-for turn of affairs does not destroy that equilibrium, then we say: "How self-possessed he is!" Take for instance, a fire: everything is going along smoothly, peacefully, and without any intimation of trouble from any source. Without warning the cry is suddenly raised: "Fire!" Immediately most people are liable to lose all sense of coolness and thought; their feelings rise even as the flames, and they may do anything but the right thing: if left to them, the fire might spread hopelessly; it is the self-possessed that are going to put it out.

When a surprise strikes the man who lacks self-possession, he says in effect: "Hurry, escape; a bombshell!" and off he flies, perhaps from the frying pan into the fire. Bewilderment follows confusion, excitement turns into chaos, and the poor fellow is at the mercy of the merest nothing. For often, in such cases, in the words of the ancient, "the mountain labors, and behold, there comes forth a mouse."

But the self-possessed man, under the same conditions, acts quite differently. He says in effect: "Ha! just what I wanted; here is a fine opportunity to get some practice." Instead of flying away, he stands his ground without flinching, cooly considers the real threats in the case, and makes ready to deal with them. Instead of being bewildered, he is collected; instead of confusion, he experiences clear-headedness; if there was any excitement, it was over in a flash, and, like a cat that is thrown from a window, he regains his equilibrium almost before he loses it, landing square on his feet, safe on "terra firma."

48

This is the natural way; fear is replaced by a certain bravery, which actually makes a joy out of the unenjoyable. Job pictures this paradox by painting a vivid picture of the war horse. "He breaketh up the earth with his hoof, he pranceth boldly, he goeth forward to meet armed men. He despiseth fear, he turneth not his back to the sword Above him shall the quiver rattle, the spear and shield shall glitter.... When he heareth the trumpet he saith: Ha, ha: he smelleth the battle afar off, the encouraging of the captains, and the shouting of the army." (Chapter 39)

But there is also a supernatural way, the way the saints usually did it. Their joy in battle was that of a soldier who is willing to do anything for his leader, as St. Paul, in his Epistle to the Romans, avers: "But in all these things we overcome because of him who has loved us." (8.37) This supernatural motive, besides containing the pure idea of love and gratitude, may also have that of penance for sin, either personal or general, or increase of eternal merit, or any other spiritual aim. This supernatural way often results in more of a paradox than even the natural way, as

St. Teresa of Avila, in one of her treatises, expresses it, using the novel term, "A glorious frenzy." Perhaps, when she wrote this, she was thinking of St. Paul's expression in his First Epistle to the Corinthians: "If any one of you thinks himself wise in this world, let him become a fool, that he may come to be wise." (3:18) For truly, unless one sees the matter in this light, he will find himself bewildered by many a passage in the Lives of the Saints.

Chapter 13

"PUT BACK THY SWORD!"

Peace-making was brought out in a very strong light when our Savior told St. Peter, who in his anger had cut off the servant's ear, to put back his sword into its place. " 'Put back thy sword into its place: for all those who take the sword will perish by the sword.' " (Matt. 26.52)

It is but natural that a peaceful man will try to make others peaceful. Not only the peace which he himself feels makes him happy, but also that which others feel. He is like a bright light, that brightens everything upon which it falls. In the first place, his facial expression possesses a power hard to resist. It is hard to put up a show of anger against a man who meets you with an unruffled countenance. For anger is fed by a return of anger; if it does not find this, it goes down like a fire without fuel. In the second place, the peaceful

man's words exert an influence that is hard
to oppose; they put passion to shame, and
are compared to oil which is poured on rag-
ing waters. In the third place, his actions
are of such a nature that excitement and
nervous commotion find themselves out of
place in their presence. It is said that serpents are handled successfully only by
those who know how to make all their
movements slow and without a jar; quick,
nervous movements render serpents liable
to strike; they hear, that is, perceive vi-
brations with their tongues, which begin to
shoot forth quickly and ominously, when
someone speaks in a loud or excited voice.

Live with wolves, and you will learn to
howl, says the old proverb. A passionate
man makes others passionate. But the opposite is also true. If you live with a mild
person, you will be inclined to become mild.
Example draws, and indeed with a gentle
force that is rather persuasion than force.

When we see that another has lost his
peace on our account, even though we are
innocent of guilt, it is our duty to do all in
our power to put him again at peace.
Otherwise we displease God, according to
our Savior, who very plainly indicated this

when He said: " 'Therefore, if thou art
offering thy gift at the altar, and there
rememberest that thy brother has anything
against thee, leave thy gift before the altar
and go first to be reconciled to thy brother,
and then come and offer thy gift.' " (Matt.
5.23-25) Both he and we will feel better,
if we do this.

Then, it is proper to recall here how
happy it makes one feel to practice the
spiritual works of mercy: to console those
under trial; to condole with the bereft; to
comfort the sorrowing; to solace the sad;
to pity the suffering; to soothe the
wounded; to intercede for the accused; all
of these are ways of restoring peace, as
far as we can, to the soul that is in straits.

It is a point of wisdom to look ahead in
regard to this virtue, and prevent, where
possible, anything that may destroy or in-
jure peace among our fellows. Harshness
is generally detrimental to the human
make-up, and where it can be avoided, why
not avoid it? Passionate zeal thinks that
the greater the jolt, the more powerful the
effect, not recollecting that the result obtained in correction is not commensurate
with the simultaneous effect obtained in

the excitement caused. If this excitement cannot be avoided, then of course it would be negligence to shun its cause; but if it can be avoided, discretion and charity would advise avoiding it. All this is particularly true where many are concerned; the greater the crowd, the greater ought to be the care. It is not pleasant to others, nor to ourselves, when we stir up unnecessary suffering.

Finally, a caution must be remembered: not to intrude where we are not wanted. Otherwise our good intentions may result in conditions becoming worse instead of better. St. Luke relates a significant instance. "Now one out of the crowd said to him, 'Master, tell my brother to divide the inheritance with me.' But he said to him, 'Man, who has appointed me a judge or arbitrator over you?'" (12.13,14) At first sight, this might look like a good opportunity to perform a charitable deed; but on second sight, we realize that our Savior acted very prudently. Such a 'charitable' deed could leave many bitter regrets in its train!

Chapter 14

ROASTING ONES EGGS

Our Savior wanted His followers to avoid all wrangling and discord among themselves; He exhorted all to preserve this mutual peace. " 'Be at peace with one another.' " (Mark 9.49)

Disputing and arguing about unimportant matters often leads to bitter quarrels and wretched discord. Some are so enamored of this characteristic, that if you take one side, they are sure to take the other. It is not so much the thing argued about that interests them; it is their own arguing about it that enthralls their attention. They trouble little about effects, just as long as they have an adversary to tilt swords with. They remind us of Bacon's description of the self-lover, who, he says, will burn down another's house, just to roast his own eggs. Or, like Richard, Duke of Gloucester, they are impatient

when things go well, and crave some dis-
agreement. "Now is the winter of our dis-
content made glorious summer by this sun
of York; and all the clouds that lour'd
upon our house in the deep bosom of the
ocean buried ... I am determined to prove
the villain and hate the idle pleasures of
these days. Plots have I laid, inductions
dangerous, by drunken prophecies, libels
and dreams, to set my brother Clarence and
the king in deadly hate the one against the
other." (Richard the Third, Act I). Note
that Richard here calls the pleasures of
peace "idle," and prefers the diabolic
pleasures of "deadly hate." How such base
pleasures plague one in the end only the
wicked know.

Families must beware of this tempting
danger. The parents should carefully avoid
wrangling, especially in the presence of
their children, lest they pass on the disease.
The children should be corrected and not
allowed to acquire the habit. St. Paul compares family discord to a dog-kennel, saying: "The whole Law is fulfilled in one
word: Thou shalt love thy neighbor as thy-
self. But if you bite and devour one an-

other, take heed or you will be consumed by one another." (Gal. 5.14,15)

Neighbors, too, must beware, and not resort to litigation. "It is altogether a defect in you," wrote St. Paul to the Corinthians, "that you have lawsuits one with another." (I. 6.7) The Canon Law of the Church desires also that lawsuits be avoided; it has in mind, of course, private lawsuits, not public ones, for in the latter the common good is at stake. Two substitutes are suggested: first, compromise, in which the parties themselves agree as to settlement; then, arbitration, in which the parties agree as to the person or persons who are to assign the terms of settlement. The ideal Christian way, the friendly way, is the first, compromise; for justice, truth, and sincerity, as taught by the Gospel, should render civil action unnecessary. Think, too, of all the trouble and worry thus averted. "An ounce of prevention is worth a pound of cure."

Chapter 15

THE ROCKS IN THE ROAD

He who is too attached to tangible things is not in a condition to be tranquil when it comes to making sacrifices. This happened to the young man who wished to follow our Lord but first desired to bury his father. "And he said to another, 'Follow me.' But he said, 'Lord, let me first go and bury my father.' But Jesus said to him, 'Leave the dead to bury their own dead.'" (Luke 9.59,60)

There are some who cannot accomplish a given task without feeling in the mood for it; they are so used to following their likes and shunning their dislikes, that the very idea of adaptation is repugnant to them. They are always upset by the unexpected. And being upset, they are unhappy. They go through this ugly experience quite often, and never seem to learn better; for every time the unexpected happens, they repeat with a sort of infallible precision. Such slaves of circumstances are truly to be pitied. They miss much of the joy of life, which consists in achievement—the doing of one's work, being on the job, and doing that work well, yes, even with pleasure. The salesman in the store who is so pre-occupied with reading a novel, that every customer irks him, is indeed a sorry example of the trade!

We read of one of the old Fathers of the Church who always kept his door ajar, so that no one might think he was so pre-occupied with his writing, that he had no time to devote to the next best visitor. He was always busy, but he considered his principal business the will of God, as it might turn out, today, this hour, this very moment, sacrificing his own desires to those of his fellows, whose servant—in imitation of Christ Himself—he strove lovingly to be. He was engaged strongly with God and his neighbor, but with himself he was disengaged.

There are women who are so engaged with their cosmetics, that they have no time to care for their children, and live a life of vexation because little Johnny wants this, little Mary—quite contrary, of course —wants that. They consider themselves martyrs to the tribulations of the household, and expect pity, pity, pity, as if they were victims of a persecution.

There are children who are so engaged with their games and play, that they have no time for study or application, and look upon books as a misfortune, as the little boy who said he wished he had hold of the fellow that invented books. They are always in misery, never knowing their lessons, and fearing to be called upon. They put everything off to the last moment, and then, like the sudden cloudburst, their meagre knowledge gained flows away as quickly as it came. They are often the State's liabilities.

There are individuals in every walk of life who are so engaged in passing pleasures and trivialities, that they are continually peeved at the thought of duty, looking upon it as a necessary evil, which plagues them, poor mortals, to their dying day. The best description of them has long since been set down in the words: "What

fools these mortals be!" For they not only
hit all the rocks in the road, but also miss
the beauties and joys of the journey.

Chapter 16

LIBERTY OR LICENSE

Those who are tied down by attachments find it difficult and often practically impossible to free themselves tranquilly at the sound of a higher call. This happened to the young man who loved his relatives more than God. "And another said, 'I will follow thee, Lord; but let me first bid farewell to those at home.' Jesus said to him, 'No one, having put his hand to the plow and looking back, is fit for the kingdom of God.'" (Luke 9. 61,62)

We are naturally liberty-loving creatures; for God made us with a free will according to His own image. But we woefully interchange the idea of true liberty with the idea of license, and fall into all sorts of abnormalities as a result. Thus the thief, seeing where he can easily pilfer a sum of money, says to himself: "I can, if I want to, I am free; why then hesitate?"

Without further thought, he obeys his impulse and takes the money. Had he stopped to think, he would have realized that, instead of being free, he was enslaving himself to a mere motion of his lower self, an unjust motion, for the money belonged to someone else, and he was not 'free' to take it. Had he resisted, he would now indeed be free, free from that impulse and its deed, which now not only enslaves him but also tortures him with the remembrance of its injustice.

This is a picture of many and many a condition in the human breast. These myriad conditions are all different in time, place, and circumstance; but in their general character they are all of the same mold—license. Most of the misery and unhappiness on the earth can be traced to these conditions. For, instead of drawing the soul closer to God, license always pulls it away the farther from Him.

Nor is it necessary that license always imply sin. The young man in the Gospel, referred to above, did not sin by loving his parents the way he did, but the love was so strong that it kept him away from something high and noble—the service of God.

Thus anyone may become so attached to a
friend or relative, that when it comes to
making an important decision affecting his
soul, he cannot bring himself to do any-
would advise, no matter what the advice
would advise, no matter what the advice
might be. Here again we have license leading to enslavement—the poor victim is a
slave to his friend or his relative; he has
sacrificed to him his freedom. In return he
gets the 'delight' of a worried conscience.

Nor is it only persons to whom the
thoughtless sacrifice their freedom; no,
they often sacrifice the same freedom to
things. Eve sacrificed it to the apple;
Adam to Eve's persuasion, and, as a result,
to the apple. The business man sees where
he can cheat a customer; he sacrifices his
freedom to that opportunity. The lustful
man sees where he can obtain a forbidden
pleasure; he sacrifices his freedom to that
disgraceful license. And thus, all through
life, true fredom is daily and hourly sacrificed to miserable license, while suffering
increases by leaps and bounds, so that
many, going mad with the torture of the
enslavement, seek to relieve themselves by
suicide.

Turn from this sad and sordid picture and look at the other. There you see human nature striving to return to its original state—before the advent of the apple. It treasures its true freedom—the right and privilege of preferring the good. It resists the temptation of license, and finds a continually growing satisfaction—the satisfaction of still being free and not enslaved to anyone or to anything. Like the man who climbs a mountain, such a soul rises ever to a more clarified and delightful atmosphere. And when he reaches at last the top—a happy death—he can say: "I have conquered—yet not I, but Christ living in me." (See Gal. 2.20) His freedom is now sealed forever.

Chapter 17

THE TREASURE OF FREEDOM

If flesh and blood stand in his way, the true Christian must decide against them in favor of Christ; for only conscience brings true peace—all other peace is a sham. " 'If anyone comes to me and does not hate his father and mother, and wife and children, and brothers and sisters, yes, and even his own life, he cannot be my disciple. And he who does not carry his cross and follow me, cannot be my disciple.' " (Luke 14. 26,27)

The word 'hate' here has the meaning of, 'hardening oneself against yielding to evil influence.' For God always comes first. Relatives are here mentioned in detail, because the difficulty is greater where they are concerned. We might, therefore, in treating of detachment, refer the term to anything or anyone which serves as a drawing-force for us away from the will of God.

The point to be stressed here is, that, no matter how great we may think the need be to preserve our social connections intact, it cannot be greater than the need to preserve our soul's connections with God. The peace which is derived from social ease and satisfaction is natural; but the peace which has its source in shaping our actions according to the divine will is supernatural. The natural, says our Savior, must give in to the supernatural; for the natural lasts only for time, the supernatural lasts for eternity. In other words, it is a question of faith in the Creator, or faith in mere creatures.

Young people ought to be detached in their choice of a mate for life, so that they make that choice according to what will result in their spiritual peace and integrity, not according to what at the moment is emotionally felt and desired. By hasty decisions many ruin their whole after life, and find themselves in the condition expressed by that belatedly wise husband who thus lamented: "I said A; now I must say B." Perhaps his wife sang the same song.

But not all young people are stung by the wedding-bug; there have always been

and there still are certain chosen souls, who
for the greater love of God, want to sacrifice their natural rights and devote themselves entirely to the needs of religion, religion understood in the personal and the
general sense. Why, says our Lord in
effect, should they be deprived of this good
and holy longing, just because some relative or relatives are opposed to their desired step? Therefore, He adds in effect
again, even though children are bound by
the Fourth Commandment, they are more
bound by the First, and as a consequence
ought to follow God's invitation even at
the expense of offending their parents, who
have no right to place themselves before
God. If parents would only stop to consider that a child's future is going to be
happy or unhappy according to conscience,
they could not dare to stand in the way. If
afterwards they realize that they have kept
their children back from a superior good,
then their own happiness is also affected.

It is wise to keep ourselves always detached from what we like or love, in so far
that we preserve our power and our rights
intact, ready to use when the time is ripe.
By not making unwise commitments of any

kind that might bind us unnecessarily, we hold to that treasure, our freedom, and thus make one of the best investments possible for our future peacefulness of soul. In these matters both our temporal happiness and our eternal form the guiding principle.

Chapter 18

"POOR PETE!"

No man is serene and happy who is dissatisfied; but our Lord said that the hankering after the passing goods of this world never truly satisfies. "And he said to them, 'Take heed and guard yourselves from all covetousness, for a man's life does not consist in the abundance of his possessions.'" (Luke 12.15)

To be enslaved is bad enough; but to be tyrannized over is much worse. The effect of this tyranny is twofold: the victim becomes vicious, as well as treacherous. For on the one hand, vice thrives as in a hotbed where money opens the way; and on the other, no one knows what to expect—often respected citizens are suddenly put in the limelight for embezzlement. And what of the soul? What kind of happiness is that where the mind is ever seeking to

70

cover up one illicit transaction by heaping on still another?

Imagine the heart of Judas. What did he care for justice, for honesty, faith, his apostolic vocation? He had succeeded in gaining a little of the filthy lucre he craved; but instead of giving him pleasure, it so sickened him, that he threw it down as if it were a nest of poisonous reptiles. But that nest of reptiles had already done its work; his heart was poisoned with despair, and he quickly went from bad to worse, ending his life with a tragedy more infamous and terrible than any before or after.

The demon surely must have had his part—and that not a little one—in the career of Judas. He had noted the Apostle's weakness, and there he gained an entrance. It is the same with anyone. Whoever notes that he has a weakness for money, let him beware; that weakness gradually will rob him of his dear soul's joy, and will plunge him into misery, unless he is careful to counteract it with the strength of virtue. The demon knows how to deceive us all, and under guise of necessity and

duty to draw us into the entangling meshes
of his infernal net.

How different is the state of soul where
a man can look back on all his money trans-
actions, and feel the satisfaction of having
acquired nothing except by honest means!
Even though he has never acquired much
of this world's goods, still the satisfaction
of soul which is his more than compensates
for his comparative lack of success. He has
been successful from God's point of view,
and as long as that is true, what does it
matter how he compares with some of his
comrades? Perhaps they, in their affluence, laugh at him and say: "Poor Pete:
there is as much business in him as in a
kitten." But he in his turn can with much
more reason laugh at them, for they are
not on the side of the good angels, but on
the side of the bad, who on Judgment Day
will laugh them to scorn for being so easily
duped. No; Pete is not as poor as they
think; in fact, he is rich, having God's
favor and the joy of a good conscience.

One of the entrances to money-misery is
very innocent-looking, and many go in
there just for the fun of the thing, but
stay in dead earnest. That fatal door is

gambling. O how many tragedies began with that sorrowful step! Such tragedies envelop not only their immediate victim, but often his dependents. Happy, thrice happy he who has consistently said 'No' to this siren. He has escaped an octopus.

Then there is another entrance to money-misery which Ben Franklin described in his own way, saying: "He who goes a-borrow-ing goes a-sorrowing." Necessary debts are bad enough, and leave in their train many tears of anguish and heart-beats full of fear and uncertainty. But it is the un-necessary debts that weigh heaviest and cause the most suffering. And the irony of it is, that often they are not the effect of an irresponsible outlook or a care-for-nothing attitude, but rather the outcome of thoughtless self-sufficiency. By not keep-ing an exact account of one's assets and liabilities, and not regulating one's budget carefully, the debts accumulate without being noticed, like moths in a neglected closet, until of a sudden the truth dawns, and then the hole-filled garments are pulled out and the losses counted, to the great dis-may and worry of the 'paterfamilias' who must labor all the harder in the sweat of his brow to make good the oversight of the forgetful wife. The 'paterfamilias' in this case is a man's good will, and the wife is his sleeping intellect.

A man who has no debts, or whose debts are at least well proportioned to his income, can sleep peacefully. When he wakes, he has not that spectre before him, which takes on various forms, now that of the collector, again that of the prosecuting lawyer, or still again that of the judge pronouncing sentence. He has been wise enough to judge himself—and incidentally his pocketbook—beforehand, so that afterward he need not fear judgment. It will be the same on Judgment Day: those with debts will be on the left side—the goats; while those without debts will find themselves on the right side—the happy elect.

Chapter 19

"THY FAITH HAS SAVED THEE!"

Over-anxiety as to our interior condition or future retribution can only be remedied by seeking the truth, or, if we have it, by trusting to it. Thus Mary Magdalene acted. "But he said to the woman: 'Thy faith has saved thee; go in peace.'" (Luke 7.50)

Judgment will come to all of us, there is no doubt about that. But there is no reason to go to excess when fearing that judgment. Fear is a salutary virtue, yet if it grows excessive, it is no longer salutary but detrimental. It may be compared to a medicine. How foolish does he show himself who, receiving a medicine from a physician with the direction to take a spoonful every hour, concludes that he will get well much more quickly if he takes the medicine every quarter of an hour.

If there is real reason for fear, we ought certainly to look into the matter, whatever it is, and try to allay that fear with good, solid arguments. If a person fears that he is not serving God in the right way, let him examine conscientiously what appears to be the right way, and then wisely follow that way. This will undoubtedly allay his fear, ease his heart, and furnish a safe and sure foundation for all his future actions. Some dilly-dally all their lives with such a fear, and even though it is well grounded, they never have the courage to allay it. Is this not foolish? It is as foolish as the course of a man would be who, having reasonable fears that his physical condition was under suspicion, would go on and on, with his symptoms always warning him, and yet never taking the time to consult a good physician. A stitch in time always saves nine!

If there is no real reason for fear, then there may be something wrong with the virtue of hope. It is not functioning as it should. With a healthy soul, hope always solves the problems as they come along. Counsel is necessary, a good will is necessary, but hope must supply what is

76

lacking in both. A man in doubt may ask the most learned theologian about that doubt, but in many cases, learned or not learned, that theologian could not answer that question with absolute certainty if he tried a whole year and consulted all the tomes ever written on the subject. Or the same man may try to prove to himself that he has done everything possible to satisfy conscience; nevertheless, with St. Paul, he can reach no more certainty than to say: "Nay I do not even judge my own self. For I have nothing on my conscience, yet I am not thereby justified; but he who judges me is the Lord." (I Cor. 4.4)

The Holy Writ always demands fear; but never in any case excessive fear. It is chiefly concerned with inspiring us with hope and confidence in God's goodness, which can make up for all deficiencies which are not certainly unamended. It is strange that a person, with excessive fear, should so often find it difficult in the extreme to have confidence in the promised mercy of God; it would seem that, instead of hesitating, he would grasp at that offered raft of safety with the greatest alacrity and with all his being. An explana-

tion of this seeming contradiction in reason
may be this: nature is too proud to acknowledge its need for help; it would much
prefer if it could say: "I know that I am
innocent—I have need of nothing else."
It is blind, however, to this pride, and does
not see that humility is the secret of true
hope. The proud Pharisee did not say:
"I *hope* that I am not like the rest of men,"
but, "I thank God that I *am not* like the
rest of men." Christ had no good words
for him; but He praised the poor publican,
who said sincerely: " 'O God, be merciful to
me the sinner!' " (Luke 18.13)

Chapter 20

A SEDATIVE POWER

Christ was always stirring up hope in
the hearts of His hearers. How often did
He not give expression to the idea of His
coming to save that which was lost! " 'The
Son of Man came to save what was lost.' "
(Matt. 18.11)

Taken from the purely natural standpoint, hope possesses a sedative power over
the many disturbances that are liable to
beset the human soul. It is a combination
virtue, composed on the one hand of desire,
and on the other of expectancy. If a man
does not desire a thing, he will not hope for
it; nor, even if he does desire it, will he
hope for it, if he has no reason to expect
it. It is the sphere of hope to look forward to the things which are not yet in our
possession, and therefore it has much to
do with our happiness; for it gives life

to our desires and fulfils them in a manner even before they are reached.

Taken from the supernatural standpoint, hope lifts us from the uncertain combination of desire and expectancy—due to the corresponding uncertainty of human foresight and ability, to the comparative certainty of assurance—due to the accepted fact that God can neither deceive nor be deceived.

We call that a forlorn hope where a person expects something natural without having any good ground for expecting it, as a sick man, whom the doctors have given up, who nevertheless looks forward to getting well. To all appearances and human experience he is doomed; he is not going to get well, but he is going to die. His hope gives him some consolation for the present, but as to the future it is worthless. The physician and his medicines have a power up to a certain point, but from there on they are impotent. However, if that person looks higher and places his hope in God's help, he is not only consoled thereby for the present, but can also look to the future with a certain degree of assurance, according to his faith, for now he is not dealing with a limited human agency, but with the divine unlimited power. The joy of his hope in increased thereby, and can be increased further still in accord with the strength of his faith, which is certainly something worth while. Moreover, the hope we place in God's help is buoyed up by the realization that, even though it is not His will to give us just what we want, He will not disappoint us, but will give us something else, if not here, then assuredly in eternity.

In this way, Christian hope becomes not simply a help, but a decidedly real possession; for it is going to lead us to something, whatever it may be, and though we must leave that something to God's decision, it *is* on the way! And the best of all is—that we ourselves are on the way.

Chapter 21

"O YOU OF LITTLE FAITH!"

Our Savior always inspired others with confidence regarding their own souls. He said, God even cares for the grass of the field, how much more for men, who, with God's help, can find all things possible. " 'If God so clothes the grass of the field, which today is alive and tomorrow is thrown into the oven, how much more you, O you of little faith!' " (Matt. 6.30) " 'With men this is impossible, but with God all things are possible.' " (Ibid. 19.26)

Confidence is the hope of a childlike soul. It is hope enlivened by a certain familiarity of approach and boldness of assurance. In the natural sphere it takes on the form of a healthy self-trust. Its opposite we often refer to as an 'inferiority complex.' There are people who are ever afraid of themselves; they are so cautious that, rather than take any risk of a mistake or wrong step, they abstain entirely from any attempt. Their false philosophy has been cleverly exposed in the common saying, 'The only man who makes no mistake is he who does nothing.' Self-confidence is what we all need, each in his way; otherwise we are mere lookers-on, not live, energetic doers.

But as much as self-confidence keeps a man in buoyant spirits, he needs also a higher confidence, in order to take care of the hard and difficult things, or, as our Lord expressed it the impossible things. This is confidence in God. We recognize that as our Creator God deserves the fullest confidence on our part; for how could He reasonably neglect to care for that which He made, or how could He possibly forget to do so? The Holy Scriptures are full of passages which inculcate this care of God for us; and it is especially impressed in the doctrine of the Guardian Angel.

There is a joy that grows out of confidence which results in the formation of a happy disposition. When this confidence is fortified by faith and elevated by noble virtue, supernaturally considered, it is stronger in the long run than any other force on earth. It encourages, it inspires, it crushes fear, it goads on to ever continuing effort until success, it banishes gloom, it establishes order, it engenders enthusiasm, and leads to final victory. Patrick Henry had it, and passed it on to others, when he uttered those immortal words to the effect that human weakness is but apparent, since there is a God above who will help us!

Chapter 22

THE HAPPY FISHERMAN

As the father of the possessed boy confidently expected help, so may we also go to Christ, and say: 'I believe, Lord, help my unbelief.' "But Jesus said to him, 'If thou canst believe, all things are possible to him who believes!' At once the father of the boy cried out, and said with tears, 'I do believe; help my unbelief.'" (Mark 9. 22, 23)

Expectancy is confidence in action, visible, audible, evident. It is illustrated in the saying of the ancient, who, when encouraging others, would merely repeat the simple words: "Cheer up! I see land." Or it is forcibly put before us in the 'tears' of the distressed father mentioned above.

Expectancy is therefore filled with earnestness. We are in search of something, and we mean to get it. It has the effect of rousing our drooping spirits, so much so that, like a flower that has wilted and is refreshed by a new supply of water, we lift our heads and breathe more easily. It makes us often just the opposite of what we were before. It re-enlivens us, it re-creates us.

There is a joy in expectancy that keeps us going. Take, for instance, the fisherman. How he can sit on the bank, hour after hour, anxiously awaiting the telltale ripple in the water. And does he enjoy it? Ask him. If he is a true fisherman, he will reply in surprise: "Well, what do you think I stay there for?" Or, take another example, with which all of us are more familiar—that of a person playing a game. How engrossed he is, oblivious to all else, watching his own moves materialize, and those of the other players. Does he enjoy it? Ask him, and he will give the same answer as the fisherman. He not only enjoys it, but he looks forward to it with avidity. The very coming of it in the future makes him happy in the present.

Apply this to daily life. Make it a fishing trip, or a game. Be always expecting something good to happen. And if it doesn't—well, rejoice in the fact that it happens to the other fellow instead of to you. If he gets the fish that you wanted, he has the joy of it; you can share his joy if you will. If he wins the game instead of yourself, don't do as so many do—frown and fret, but say: "I can't win all the time; I am glad his time came; I rejoice with him." In this way we may habitually be as happy in our way as the fisherman or the gamester is in his; and that is no mean gain!

Chapter 23

FAST COLOR

Those who take spirituality seriously are the only ones who can successfully preserve self-control against all odds. Tortures and death cannot dislodge them. " 'Be on your guard. For they will deliver you up to councils, and you will be beaten in synagogues and you will stand before governors and kings for my sake, for a witness to them.' " (Mark 13.9)

"Don't be so serious!" How often this phrase is used. If it is meant to call one's attention to a long face, vinegar eyes, and puckered lips, then its propriety can scarcely be called in question; for such seriousness does no one good. However, it is only too often meant to point out one's fidelity to God's ordinances, and then its impropriety is evident.

Serious people look at everything according to its importance. Their duty to serve

God and give Him His due they place above all else. Nor does this serious aspect which they have of life rob them of true joy and cheer. On the contrary, it increases their happiness, and therefore their geniality.

There have been martyrs who remained even exteriorly cheerful under the most excruciating tortures, for instance, St. Lawrence, who, while being roasted on a gridiron, said to his executioner: "Turn me over on the other side; this one is now well done."

Indeed, it is the man who is truly serious who retains his peace and joy under pressure. The other fellow, who was always bubbling over with gaity, begins to wince and claw like a teased animal. The one has fast color, which does not fade in the rain; the other, after being drenched, has quite a different shade!

Another point is this: there are some people who laugh at the idea of a devil—that part of dogma is not to be taken seriously, according to their all-knowing wisdom. But the truly serious man does take the devil not only seriously, but most seriously. He believes the words of St. Peter:

"Be sober, be watchful! for your adversary the devil, as a roaring lion, goes about seeking someone to devour. Resist him, steadfast in the faith." (I. 5. 8,9)

Chapter 24

PILGRIMAGES TO THE PAST

Christian gravity is the highest ideal before us, be it of soul or manner. What we are before God and how He will judge us in the end is the all-important thing in life. " 'But take heed to yourselves, lest your hearts be overburdened with self-indulgence and drunkenness and the cares of this life, and that day come upon you suddenly as a snare.' " (Luke 21. 34,35)

Having a good time, in the worldly sense, is often considered happiness. Eating, drinking, enjoying social prestige, and the like natural pleasures, these things are looked upon not only as signs of happiness, but even as the essential condition. Rich men are envied, because their wealth places at their disposal these pleasures. Pleasure ought to be lasting in order to be true; otherwise it has a flaw. And often, it is not only not lasting, but even turns into its

91

opposite. The pleasure of virtue is alone lasting, and for that reason the virtuous man is really happy, whereas the man of passing pleasure is happy only temporarily and as a result of the exterior and not of the interior. Therefore, the advice of our Lord, in the text above, is not just good, but it is the best possible.

The word 'gravity' in the usual sense means, the natural force that pulls everything material downward. In our present sense it means, the supernatural force that pulls spiritual things upward. In other words, a man who is grave is elevated in thought, upright in word, and noble in deed. And as the former kind of gravity keeps everything in place on the earth, so this kind keeps everything spiritual in place, the soul, the mind, the imagination, the passions. It therefore attains to good order, and as a consequence to peace, and —what is still more—to genuine happiness.

Understood in this manner, true gravity is something essentially joyful and full of interior poise. It fails to come up to this ideal only if there is some flaw in its make-up. When a person, instead of thinking back over his past ugly things, which include his failings, his blunders,—those sores that leave such hideous scars, and his other unpleasant experiences—such as horrid dreams and morbid pictures, does so only in a general way (having already specifically repented of them, perhaps long, long ago, so as to regret them indeed, be sorry for them, and be resolved not to repeat them) such a procedure increases his joy, for with St. Paul he can say: "But one thing I do: forgetting what is behind, I strain forward to what is before, I press on towards the goal, to the prize of God's heavenly call in Christ Jesus." (Phil. 3.13,14) On the other hand, if he is forever repeating in his mind those ugly things of the past, he is always irritating his memory, and as a result is always in a potential state of chagrin, which quite naturally robs him of the peace which he might otherwise have, since every time he places himself in the same conditions he suffers the same misery. Why do this? Does God require it? Is it really enjoyable or profitable? According to St. Paul, it is neither one nor the other. "Forgetting what is behind,"—those are his exact words. After we have tried to make amends for spilling the milk, there is no use in making a pilgrimage very now and then to the spot, in order to contemplate the catastrophe. Our whole life is full of such spots; it is enough that they have not proved our ruin; for the rest there is no sense in letting them prove our chronic misery.

Chapter 25

"SOME TRUST IN CHARIOTS"

True cheerfulness, as has been pointed out more than once in these pages, depends on the faith which we have in divine Providence, as our Savior said, when He spoke of the ravens. "But he said to his disciples: 'Therefore I say to you, do not be anxious for your body, what you shall put on. The life is a greater thing than the food, and the body than the clothing. Consider the ravens: they neither sow nor reap, they have neither storeroom nor barn; yet God feeds them. Of how much more value are you than they!'" (Luke 12.22-24)

Cheerfulness is something positive; it is not only the result of a condition, but it is a condition itself—an acquired condition. For everyone can make himself cheerful on occasion, at least exteriorly. Thus a man expresses his good cheer to a dog—with a smile and greeting; even the dog is able to return that good cheer—with wagging of his tail and pawing his master.

But there is a difference between mere natural cheerfulness and supernatural cheerfulness. The latter is founded on faith in that universal care emanating from the divine power—the care of the Creator for His creatures; and it is that faith which, being something positive, can be increased always, with a corresponding increase in its effect—supernatural cheerfulness.

The soul that is filled with this realization is wrapped, as it were, in a continual atmosphere of elevating and solacing cheer. It is the atmosphere of confidence, safety, protection. Suppose, for instance, that a father tells his wife that he is going to take her little child out for a walk; how satisfied and free of worry the mother is, knowing that the little one could not be better taken care of! But, if the little child were to go out on the street by itself, that mother would be full of fear till it returned safely; for she would not have the consolation of relying on adequate protection.

Faith grows in the soul, just as a tree in the soil, and as it grows it brings forth fruit, which is delightful to eat. The consciousness of the divine protection is one of the sweetest fruits in all the spiritual garden, and besides being sweet is most nourishing to the inner man. Moreover, it is one of the easiest fruits to cultivate, given the proper climate, which must be a warm one, that is, one imbued with the heat of loving emotion; for where a soul does not try to feel the divine presence diffusing itself throughout creation, there this fruit will find difficulty in maturing. In some it is nipped already in the bud by the cruel frost of doubt and weakened belief. Poor mortals! They do not know what real joy they are missing.

"Some trust in chariots, and some in horses: but we will call upon the name of the Lord our God. They are bound, and have fallen; but we are risen, and are set upright." So sings the psalmist. (19.8.9)

Chapter 26

HURT FEELINGS

In the Lord's Prayer we pray for our daily bread, but we preface the petition with an act of resignation, asking that the will of God be done on earth as it is in heaven. " 'Thy will be done on earth, as it is in heaven.' " (Matt. 6.10)

Hurt feelings are always hard to overcome, because they are generally inflicted by a friendly source, from a source which we thought could do only good to us; but besides being hard to overcome, they make us often extremely unhappy. A girl, for instance, who thinks she is very beautiful, is told by her bosom girl friend that it would be very much to her advantage if she would improve her looks. What a thunderbolt, right out of the clear sky! She must now readjust herself to an entirely new idea, and a very unpleasant one at that. Yes, if she does not want to be foolish, she must resign herself to the fact that she is not so attractive in others' eyes as she had thought. She had always considered herself a very rare bird; now she must go down a few notches and believe that she is not even a very good common one. It takes all her power of good sense not to be resentful, or even revengeful. And as to preventing the misery it has all caused, she simply can't do it.

The world is full of such examples of hurt feelings, where comparatively petty affairs keep rankling in the interior and ruin one's days and nights. Natural resignation is the cure for this condition; it would teach the victim not to make a mountain out of a molehill, nor to find consolation in one's mistaken ideas, especially after they have been pointed out. It would urge adaptation and a more sane view of everything in closer agreement with common sense. It would suggest that the hurt feelings might be changed into glad feelings, on the ground that some good correction has come to one, as the old saying puts it: "Give special attention to what people say when they are angry at you; for they have a reason for saying it."

As in the natural life, so in the supernatural one; we are inclined to be hurt, as it were, if God does not give us just what we want, and even feel like saying, or perhaps even say it: "And I prayed *so hard.*" Though we do not like, perhaps, to acknowledge it, we are secretly peeved at our being left in the ante-room, as it were, and decide to show our resentment at such neglect by leaving altogether, carrying away with us, of course, a bosom full of pouting emotions, that henceforward plague us and torture us with impunity. We say in effect with the old fellow in the story: "I prayed once a whole day for something and didn't get it. Prayer is all humbug—humbug I say." And with that poor comfort we forsake the very thing that could help us.

A person ought to realize that resignation is one of the conditions of true prayer and trust in God. For, although He promised to hear us, He did not promise to hear us just as soon as we would like or in the way we would like. He will undoubtedly hear us, but in His own good time and way—which is always the best for us, we may be sure. Therefore the true Christian remains cheerful, whether he gets just what he wants when he wants it, or not. "God knows best" is his ever-ready motto.

Chapter 27

"GOD WILLING!"

We may hope to obtain from God whatever we think is good, but never without the proviso, 'God willing.' Jesus Himself did this, when He said to His Father, 'As Thou wilt.' " 'Father, if it is possible, let this cup pass away from me; yet not as I will, but as thou willest.' " (Matt. 26.39)

A man gets much more real cheer out of conforming himself to the inevitable than by seeking out what crumbs of comfort he can find in sulking. For such conformity to God's will is one of the best virtues anyone can practice. It furnishes the assurance of pleasing God more than anything else could, since it is a proof of one's love for God. The theologians define such love as "union of man's will with that of God."

This conformity of oneself to the higher power is not practiced just when it is needed, but all the time. The soul is in a perpetual state of conforming itself. Hence the cheer that results is something not for the occasion but becomes a deep habit. The frown of dissatisfied nature changes into the smile of nature clarified. And that smile so belongs to the man that it is associated with him in the minds and memories of all who come in contact with him. People say: "He always has a smile for you." Even in the midst of trouble and pain, such a person can still exhibit a smiling countenance. And this smile in turn works in its own way, affecting the soul of the individual concerned with an ever stronger influence. Nor is it a forced smile. He smiles because he is always satisfied and happy; and he is the more satisfied and happy because he smiles; even a forced smile will make us feel better for the moment. Neither is this smile merely for others; no, even when alone, he smiles to himself. But above all, he smiles to God, anxious always to assure Him that, whatever may happen, good or evil, pleasant or unpleasant, desirable or undesirable, it will always be taken humbly as from the divine hand—a gift more valuable than anything else earth could offer.

St. Paul used the expression, 'God will-ing.' And after his example many use it habitually, not only in mind and heart, but in word and writing. Such can be depended upon not to be grouches. They see the good side of every situation, and try to make the most of the bad side. The more these people increase and their opposites de-crease, the better off the world will be, for it will be a happier world.

Chapter 28

SPARROWS AND FALLING HAIRS

Sincere abandonment of ourselves to God's care is the only real remedy for human fear. Our Savior reminded us of how God protects the little sparrows—how much more ourselves? " 'Are not five sparrows sold for two farthings? And yet not one of them is forgotten before God. Yes, the very hairs of your head are all numbered. Therefore do not be afraid, you are of more value than many sparrows.' " (Luke 12.6,7)

In speaking of abandoning ourselves to God's Providence there are three angles to be considered: first, the angle of the past; then, that of the present; finally, that of the future. As to the past, we must avoid living in it; for this prevents us from living in the present and appreciating new things as they come along. Some are forever deploring the passing of the good old days; and therefore they are always dissatisfied with the inevitable fresh and novel blossoms of the present. Of what use is it to shed tears over the withered flowers of last year? Be one of the rest, not an ancient. Be moving, be appreciative, be progressive; there is more real happiness in this than in sitting cozily in the arm-chair of long ago and dreaming pipe-dreams, that are only useless memories, and perhaps not only useless, but even harmful.

As to the angle of the present, it is good to be like persons who ride in an airplane. It is true, accidents happen; but being in the care of a good pilot gives assurance. Now, when it comes to God, we know that He is a pilot absolutely trustworthy, both as to His knowledge and power, as also to His intention and desire. We are in His hands, and therefore we cannot suffer evil; it would be contrary to His very essence to really hurt us. We glide along, enjoying our ride to the utmost, like little babes in their buggies, worrying over nothing, confident of everything.

As to the angle of the future, a person accustomed to abandonment avoids too great a care. This pervades all his words and actions. He does not speak nervously and, as it were, in a stumbling manner, as if he had only a minute or two in which to say something; neither does he write in this manner, as some do, who get into the habit of scribbling so fast, that no one can make out their hieroglyphics. His actions, too, are measured and natural, not a hastening hither and thither, a knocking down this thing and that, a slamming of doors, a cyclonic upheaval. He abandons himself to the future in peace and joy, breathing each breath as it is given to him—a perpetual example of the old saying, "All things come to him who waits. Especially as to the future of his soul is he calm and collected, knowing that he is in the hands of the Divine Lover, who will take care of him, bringing him safely through life's vicissitudes to the last day of his journey, then transporting him safely to the great beyond. Happy? Yes, he is truly happy, even though he has trials; the trials only make him happier, because he attributes everything to God; he says: "Let them come, either the good Lord sends them or He allows them; in any case He is with them, they will only benefit me; I thank Him for them."

Chapter 29

THE REWARD IS GREAT

True joy, as Christ saw it, consists not so much in having present good things as in the confidence of one day possessing eternal good things. " 'Rejoice on that day and exult, for behold your reward is great in heaven.' " (Luke 6.23)

The divine Providence extends itself not only to this life, but aims especially at providing for our hapiness in the next life, that is, considering our innate weakness and foolish, stubborn self-will, which always wants to resist. For, in doing this, it does not offer us false food—the decoying joys of the senses, but seeks to steel us against the vicissitudes and trials that daily beset our journey to heaven. In this spirit we read with great comfort the words of St. James in the beginning of his Epistle: "Esteem it all joy, my brethren, when you fall into various trials, knowing that the trying of your faith begets patience. And let patience have its perfect work, that you may be perfect and entire, lacking nothing." St. Paul's words, too, we treasure, more than the tomes of all the philosophers: "He has said to me: 'My grace is sufficient for thee, for strength is made perfect in weakness.' Gladly therefore I will glory in my infirmities, that the strength of Christ may dwell in me." (II Cor. 12.9) The strength of Christ—what is it? " 'He who does not take up his cross and follow me, is not worthy of me.' " (Matt. 10.38)

How miserable are those poor slaves, often found in the world, who are always groping for the answer to life! "What is it all about?" they cry. They read volumes, they write long articles, they search all corners, only they pass by the real answer. And that is the answer possessed by the Christian, as delineated above, and which gives his heart so much satisfaction and assurance, peace, joy, and admirable contentment in the midst of tribulation.

Why does the aforesaid worldling not find that answer? Because he has not the insight to appreciate its wisdom. He has not the faith on which it is founded. **You** offer him, as it were, a handful of black earth; but he turns away offended, not realizing that out of that black, unsightly earth, if he would only plant the seed, would spring forth the most beautiful flower, the flower of true joy, of temporal and eternal happiness. And thus it comes, that the wise of this world never make their fellows wiser, for it is written: "'If a blind man guide a blind man, both fall into a pit.'" (Matt. 15.14)

Chapter 30

"THOU FOOL!"

Christian gladness comes from true self-restraint in this life; unbridled self-indulgence can never reach it. In the story of Dives our Savior impressed this truth most earnestly. " 'The land of a certain rich man brought forth abundant crops. And he began to take thought with himself, saying: What shall I do, for I have no room to store my crops? And he said: I will do this: I will pull down my barns and build larger ones, and there I will store up all my grain and my goods. And I will say to my soul, Soul, thou hast many good things laid up for many years; take thy ease, eat, drink, be merry. But God said to him, Thou fool, this night do they demand thy soul of thee; and the things that thou hast provided, whose will they be? So is he who lays not up treasure for himself, and is not rich as regards God.'" (Luke 12, 16-21)

The world tries its best to escape life's adversities, and it wonders at the fervent Christian, as pointed out in the foregoing chapter, for his seeming folly in patiently bearing up through it all; but when that world sees the Christian even seeking hardships and willingly taking upon himself acts of self-denial, then it throws up its hands in disgust and pity and calls him a fool. For it looks no deeper than the thing itself, and stops short of the philosopher's stone—that precious stone called "Why?"

Self-restraint was taught even by the heathen philosophers—but for the natural motive; the Christian does not stop here—he goes deeper, and perfects that natural motive by the supernatural one—again eternity. Eternity in fact is his guiding star, by which he solves all the puzzles of time. The man with the purely natural outlook appreciates the hard things of life as long as those hard things form good policy for his temporal well-being—economy, provision, discipline, and other names he gives the procedure; but when those hard things start to step on his selfish toe, he cries out in anguish and strikes the offender with his fist. And it is nothing to be wondered at; for he has little and weak faith in eternity; he is infected more or less with the plague which devastates earth with alarming increase, the dreadful plague of animalism—that plague which turns the noblest minds into the brains of mere beasts, satisfied with hay and straw, labor and upkeep, daylight and darkness, stable and field, procreation and then death without further hope, eternal nothing, everlasting stillness, unending idleness.

How can such an outlook upon life satisfy even a child, that still sees the possible? No, it will say, I am not a beast, I am not a mere temporality, I am destined for immortality, I must, I will live forever. And this little child develops into a man or woman, not doomed by infidelity's plague, but healthy and strong in the possession of vivifying nature, protecting grace, and rejoicing in that hope, which, thank God, still "springs eternal in the human breast."

Men and women of God! let those poor victims of the plague cry out with their lamentations and distressing woes, they are in the minority; let us, whose lungs are lustier, cry out the louder and drown their pessimistic dirge with the glorious Allelujas of Easter, so that all the world may hear them, and let us add the mighty words of St. Paul: "If you have risen with Christ, seek the things that are above, where Christ is seated at the right hand of God. Mind the things that are above, not the things that are of earth." (Col. 3.1-2) Let the cries of our gladness be so loud that they will not only drown out all else, but will also vibrate to the very hearts of our poor deluded brethren, reawakening music on the harps of their immortal souls!

Chapter 31

THE ONLY DOOR

Contentment is not mere enjoyment; the only door leading to it is doing the will of God as far as we know it. God alone can make us happy, nothing else; seek Him first, said Christ. " 'Seek the kingdom of God, and all these things shall be given you besides.' " (Luke 12)

There are different kinds of contentment. First, there is the contentment of the cow on the meadow, grazing slowly and leisurely, then lying down to chew her cud; she wants nothing else, and needs nothing else, for God created her precisely and only for that simple and uneventful existence. Such contentment is good, as far as it goes.

Then there is the contentment of lower nature. A man lives just as his natural instincts dictate; he troubles no one and is troubled by no one. Evil he avoids only in so far as it keeps him free of present and immediate dangers. He enjoys his body, and his body enjoys him. Such contentment is base and unworthy—unworthy of a creature made to the image and likeness of God; for it leaves one half of his being entirely neglected. He is like an apple, pleasant enough to look at on the outside, but within full of rottenness and worms and totally good for nothing.

Lastly, there is the contentment of higher nature—that part of man which is seated in his three noble and Godlike faculties, memory, intellect, and will. His memory is content, because it does not cast aside the recollection of duty, always suggested faithfully by conscience; his intellect is content, because it tries to understand that duty as well as it can, in order to fulfill it as well as it can; and his will is content, because it is really busy carrying out what the intellect suggests. Such contentment is the only real contentment, and alone worthy of the name.

The cow has pleasure; the man enjoying his lower nature has delight; but the noble individual always reaching up into the branches and possibilities of his higher nature has something which is greater than either pleasure or delight; he has satisfaction, that inner treasure which alone forms the foundation of true contentment. He has all he can have; not only half of the possible, but the whole.

However, we must remember that the reaching of this contentment is not something simple and free of hindrance. "There's many a slip 'twixt the cup and the lip," says the proverb; and thus also there are many possibilities besetting a man's path upward, which, if he is not on his guard, will spoil his chances of success. What are they? Read over the chapters of this book, and you will have a whole row of them. Mark well the ones that strike home, beware of them, and try to replace them by their opposites.

Chapter 32

THE TWO EYES OF CHRIST

Faith and morality are the two eyes with which we see as Jesus saw; without them we cannot reach His spirit, hence cannot be truly happy, no matter what we may enjoy. "Jesus therefore said to the Jews who had come to believe in him, 'If you abide in my word, you shall be my disciples indeed, and you shall know the truth, and the truth shall make you free.'" (John 8.31,32)

Among those who follow conscience there are three kinds of individuals. The first stress faith, but their morals are often out of accord. The second stress morals, but their faith is often weak and indefinite. The third stress both faith and morals, and they are examples of the· "He who is just lives by faith" of the Holy Writ. (Hab. 2.4: Rom. 1.17) For they put into practice what they believe, so that their faith becomes living in them, and can be seen in their actions and perceived in their words. The truth makes them free, that is, happy, as Christ said, and this happiness is genuine, in comparison with which all other kinds of happiness fade into nothingness.

To believe firmly and fully gives a man a certain joy which unbelievers know nothing about; that little imitation of joy which the latter have is like a false gem, which glitters, but is worth nothing. And what is the joy of believing? It is that joy obtained through the consciousness that one is not deceived. A person has little joy in making a business transaction with a man who, he has reason to fear, may cheat him. But with a friend business becomes a pleasure. God can neither deceive nor be deceived, and if we take His word, definitely and fully, for granted, we experience the joy of assurance.

Furthermore, to know that one is not just believing, but is actually putting into reality what he believes, gives him the joy of the promise; for God has attached great and incomparable promises to all His ordinances. We are not just performing a task; we are also earning very substantial wages!

In closing this chapter, let us remind ourselves that this true idea of Christian happiness does not preclude the enjoyment of the usual pleasures of life, provided they do not go to excess or are not incompatible with faith or morals. However, we must, according to St. Paul, if we do not want to lose much of the joy of true happiness, be careful to rise to the supernatural and not remain with the natural. "Therefore, whether you eat or drink, or do anything else, do all for the glory of God." (I. Cor. 10.31) In other words, if we try always to have a good intention in our enjoyments, we may take to ourselves the pleasures God gives us in our state of life, without the fear of losing our peace of heart or of offending God thereby.

Chapter 33

IN SQUALLS

The freedom derived from truth insures peace of heart. Its possessor finds no difficulty in relaxing even in the midst of noise, as Jesus on the storm-tossed ship. "And there arose a great squall, and the waves were beating into the boat, so that the boat was now filling. And he himself was in the stern of the boat, on the cushion, asleep." (Mark 4. 37,38)

It is not easy for human nature to adapt itself perfectly to all the changes which occur in daily life. The soul is affected, *nolens volens*. Somehow on a rainy day one does not feel the same as he does on a sunny day; when a headache assails him he feels decidedly different than when his head is clear and alert; it is quite an easy matter to sit down and enjoy life when the sky is cloudless, but an altogether different one to do the same when it is spitting fire

121

in every direction. To be able to weather all vicissitudes and still retain one's composure, that is something precious to possess, though not as impossible to attain as it seems.

Our Saviour, in His human nature, was of course master of all emotion. Therefore, when the storm arose on the sea, instead of growing excited, He merely slept on, which undoubtedly added greatly to His prestige with the apostles, for it was just another proof of His divine mission and messiahship. And undoubtedly, too, the great contrast between Him and themselves thus put in the limelight served to goad them on to further imitation of Him, so that they might also gradually become masters of the changing earthly journey which we call life.

Like the apostles, all of us may learn this lesson; for all of us need it, some more, some less. With some of us it is a question of the heart; if our heart is not right with God, changes about us may excite fear, suspicion, or other disturbing feelings in our interior, which will naturally also spread to our exterior. With others, it is a question of the mind; if our mind is not trained to peace and Christian poise, then certainly, though our heart is right with God, we nevertheless suffer shock, and are overwhelmed with nervous tension. With others again, it is a question of both: the heart is guilty, and the mind is upset and uncontrolled. Such are in a piteous state indeed, and suffer intensely, even though they may strive to cover it all up with a bold smile.

Would it not pay anyone, to whatever of these three classes he may belong, to take stock of his condition, and say to himself: "The years are passing over my head; it is time I am looking into my weak points before they get the better of me"? Salutary fear, even of the physical effects of such conditions, has been the beginning of many a one's change—from uneasiness to restfulness, from fear to confidence, from a perpetual state of tension to a habit of commanding self-control.

Chapter 34

HEIRS TO A KINGDOM

Christ showed us how to reach the ideal;
He told us that His Father had given us a
kingdom, and therefore not to fear. That
kingdom is the hope of the eternal reward.
" 'Do not be afraid, little flock, for it has
pleased your Father to give you the kingdom.' " (Luke 12.32)

The expression of Christ, 'kingdom,' is
interpreted as meaning not only the kingdom itself, which of course is the final
meaning, but especially a state of mind in
those who, by their lives and faith, are
destined for it. When we speak of the everlasting kingdom, heaven, we have in mind
a place of utter perfection, with nothing to
disturb, and everything to please. Therefore, to live in hope of this blessed and
eternal dwelling-place, requires a state of
mind which is, as it were, a little, though
imperfect, replica of the real thing.

St. Paul uses the sentence, "Our citizenship is in heaven." (Phil. 3.20) By this he says in effect: "During this life we get our first papers entitling us to the privilege of citizenship in that blessed land; at death we shall get our final papers, and then the matter is sealed forever." An alien seeking to become a citizen of a country, feels good when he obtains his first papers, for they are the entrance, the assurance, the promise of the final papers, which, if in the meantime he gives evidence of all that is expected of him, will undoubtedly come to him in due season. He already feels settled in hope.

Why therefore fear, except that by ill appreciation of the promise received, we forfeit the privilege we have obtained? But there is not so much danger of us forfeiting it, since we are only too glad to have what we have. In order to keep it we are willing to do anything even as a soldier who is willing to suffer, yea, to die for his fatherland; or as the mere citizen, who will stand by the soldier with all his moral and material support. The "tene quod habes" (Hold fast what thou hast) of the Apocalypse (3.11) is our battle-cry, and when the enemy would hold forth any tempting bait for desertion, that battle-cry arises from our lips, and our eyes are lifted aloft, while we add the prayerful hope of the psalmist: "My eyes are ever towards the Lord: for he shall pluck my feet out of the snare." (Ps. 24.15) He who rules our heavenly fatherland, He is our sufficiency; His kingdom is our strength, His friendship our pledge of safety!

Chapter 35

THE BEST AND THE WORST

Mary Magdalene was assured that her many sins were forgiven, because her love was so great. By a great sacrifice she reached great hope; she had real reason to be optimistic. " 'Her sins, many as they are, shall be forgiven her, because she has loved much.' " (Luke 7.47)

Optimism is an expression meaning—the habit of looking at the best side of things. It comes from the Latin, 'optimus,' which means best. Its opposite is pessimism, the meaning of which is—the habit of looking at the worst side of things.

Unforgiven sin will keep us out of heaven —that is sure; but if it has been forgiven, there is no reason for us to fear it any longer as an obstacle to our salvation. That is what spiritual optimism signifies. It is that optimism which all of us, according to the Gospel, should have; the more we have sinned, the more of it we need. Why not take it? It is offered. For the price of love it is ours.

The point here in question may be illustrated by a figure from real life. Suppose a man has been in a head-on collision; his car is demolished, and there he himself lies, bleeding, bruised, unconscious, but not yet dead. An ambulance quickly bears him to a hospital. The doctors shake their heads. "Pretty bad!" is their laconic comment. However, he is soon on the operating table, the keen knives are busy, the stiches follow, the bandages are put in place. Then, in an hour or so, he opens his eyes. His first thought is: "At least I am still alive." Some time passes, and one fine day sees him leave that hospital and enter once more into his former life. He is congratulated on his close escape, and with reason; for he is rehabilitated. The broken bones are as good as ever, the scars have healed, and all in all he is practically the same as before.

Those who have really experienced such a close escape will be the better able to appreciate the description; yet all of us, though not physically, can look back on some happening which proved a real catastrophe for our person. Perhaps we can look back on more than one, even as some people can look back on an accident here, an accident there, and an accident at the other place. Yet, like them, we have been rehabilitated, and we are none the worse for it.

Now suppose, when that sower of wild oats crashed, those who came around would have said: "There's no use trying; let him die, then bury him," and would have really carried out such pessimistic words. Impossible, you say; no one could be so cruel, and if he could be, the law would prosecute him. Well, be it so. But that is just the way scrupulous people speak and feel; yes, even after they have been rehabilitated, they keep on speaking and feeling that way. Foolish? Yes, thrice foolish. If Mary Magdalene had felt that way, she would never have sought our Lord; even after He forgave her, she would still have said: "There's no use trying: I am doomed." But she was not foolish, she was wise, and like a shrewd merchant who survives a loss, she began afresh and made the best of the situation. Posterity does not call her just

Mary Magdalene, but St. Mary Magdalene. Why should not anyone be eager to follow her example? Anyone can love God just as she did, and so be reinstated just as she was reinstated. Love can remedy all soul injuries.

Chapter 36

WRITTEN IN HEAVEN

True Christian joy is the same as that which shall be in the soul's possession in heaven, as Christ hinted when He told His disciples to rejoice that their names were written in heaven. " 'Rejoice in this, that your names are written in heaven.' " (Luke 10.20)

Whatever else heaven will have to offer, of this we are sure, it will give us the possession of God, irrevocably and forever, with all that such an infinite advantage means. The beatific vision we call it; all else that we can say of the blessed abode of the elect limps in comparison. On account of that were we created, and to that do we tend; and in that alone can we ever reach real satisfaction.

On this earth we have God, too; for if we are in His friendship, we possess Him in a manner Himself. And this joy is es-

sentially the same as that which heaven
holds out; only in heaven it will be purged
of all dross and will be everlasting, impossible to lose.

Take the case of a rich heir, not yet of
age, a boy in his 'teens. It is told him how
much his fortune will be when he is of
age, and that excites in him a continual
pleasantness of thought and feeling. But
more; he is given an allowance even beforehand, which is a little taste of the whole,
and which is in reality no different in essence.

Thus do we, who are heirs of heaven, feel
a certain flush of joy arise in our breast
whenever we think of what is coming to
us; every blessing we enjoy here makes us
think of those we shall enjoy in the happy
hereafter. If God is so good to us here,
how exceedingly good will His bounty be in
eternity! Thus do we cry out to Him in
the words of the psalmist: "Thou art my
hope, my portion in the land of the living!"
(Ps. 141.6) With St. Paul we say: "The
Spirit himself gives testimony to our spirit
that we are sons of God. But if we are
sons, we are heirs also: heirs indeed of
God and joint heirs with Christ." (Rom. 8.

16,17) And again: "Sealed with the Holy
Spirit of the promise, who is the pledge
of our inheritance, for a redemption of possession, for the praise of his glory." (Eph.
1.13,14) Or still again: "Heirs in the hope
of life everlasting." (Tit. 3.7)

And when the demon tries to destroy our
hope, mocking us with our weakness, we
answer him in the words of St. James:
"Has not God chosen the poor of this world
to be rich in faith and heirs of the kingdom
which God has promised to those who love
him?" (2.5) Or in those of St. Peter:
("Not through us, but) through the resur-
rection of Jesus Christ; who is at the right
hand of God, swallowing up death that we
might be made heirs of eternal life; for
he went into heaven, Angels, Powers and
Virtues being made subject to him." (I.
3.22)

It was St. Teresa of Avila who rejoiced
every time she perceived that another hour
had passed. "Now," she would exclaim, "I
am an hour nearer heaven." In that spirit
we spend our days, our months, our years,
our life, and when at last kind death comes
to deliver us and end our exile we say in
the words of Isaias the Prophet: "Lo, this

is our God, we have patiently waited for him, we shall rejoice and be joyful in his salvation." (25.9)

And as we stand at last before that long-awaited gate, it shall open, and our loving Savior shall stand before us, inviting us and saying: "Come, blessed of my Father, take possession of the kingdom prepared for you from the foundation of the world!" (Matt. 25.34) And going in, we shall go out no more, happy forever through all eternity, with our Father, at home where we belong!

Chapter 37

WHERE IS YOUR HEART?

The Christian's heart is enthusiastic over the possibilities of eternity, exulting in the reward that is coming. Christ exhorted us to sacrifice everything else rather than that. " 'Sell what you have, and give alms. Make for yourselves purses, that do not grow old, a treasure unfailing in heaven, where neither thief draws near nor moth destroys. For where your treasure is, there your heart also will be.' " (Luke 12. 33,34)

How the heart of a merchant rejoices when he finds that an article he is selling proves very popular; he hardly needs to find customers; all are so anxious to have that article, that they come to him before he can approach them, so that he is, as we say, swamped with orders. And what is it that makes him so happy, transported, as it were, above himself with joy? It is the fact that he has a practically limitless field. If these people want it, all other people will want it. And in fact, is not this just the way a millionare is made? Some business man finds his field—universal desire—and his profits keep on increasing and increasing.

Behold here a faint view of heaven's possibilities. It will give us God, the Infinite, of Whom we shall always and forever learn more and more; we, being finite, can never for all eternity fathom Him completely; He, being infinite, has more to give us than we can ever take in. "Behold, God is great, exceeding our knowledge: the number of his years is inestimable." (Job 36.26) "'I am the Alpha and the Omega, the beginning and the end,' says the Lord God, 'who is and who was and who is coming, the Almighty.'" (Apoc. 1.8) "To him who thirsts I will give of the fountain of the water of life, freely. He who overcomes shall possess these things, and I will be his God, and he shall be my son." (Ibid. 21. 6, 7)

What more can we say? Describe God and His infinity? Even Holy Writ does not attempt that. "'Eye has not seen nor ear heard, nor has it entered into the heart of man, what things God has prepared for those who love him.' " (I Cor. 2.9) With St. Paul let us be content to exult in hope and to say: "For the rest, there is laid up for me a crown of justice, which the Lord, the just Judge, will give to me in that day; yet not to me only, but also to those who love his coming." (II. Tim. 4.8) Not you and I; but we—all of us—are destined for eternal bliss. Happy, happy thought! Let us by all means reach it!

TOPICAL INDEX BY CHAPTERS